Book Description

Does the stock market seem incomprehensible to you? Do you curl into a ball of fear every time you hear the word "stock" or "shares"?

The stock market is one of the best ways to build wealth, but as you probably know by now, investing successfully is easier said than done.

What if there was a simple and easy-to-understand guide that demystified the market and gave you everything you needed to succeed?

In *Stock Market: Investing Guide for Beginners*, veteran investor Easton Ziegler cuts through the fog and gives you the facts in easily understood language. You'll learn how the market works and how you can position yourself to make how much money you wish to make.

In addition to this, you'll also learn about:

- Which market instruments to avoid if you want to make money
- The best passive investing strategy—make money without lifting a finger!
- How to build your portfolio for optimal performance
- The three mistakes you need to avoid at all costs
- What you need to do to unearth the next great stock—it's simpler than you think!

...and so much more!

Stop sitting on the sidelines and letting opportunity pass you by. Fear is temporary once you educate yourself. You don't need any special information or insider access to make millions in the stock market.

Click buy now!

Table of Contents

Introduction
   Passive, Active, and Everything in Between
Chapter 1: How Stock Markets Work
   Short Term or Long Term?
   Why Does the Stock Market Exist?
      Stock Exchanges
      Regulation
      Brokers
      Instruments
Chapter 2: The Five Principles of Intelligent Investing
   The First Principle
   The Second Principle
   The Third Principle
   The Fourth Principle
   The Fifth Principle
Chapter 3: The Best Passive Investing Strategy
   Passive Investing Origins
      The First Passive Investing Instrument
      What Should You Track?
   Generating Cash Flow
Chapter 4: Building a Portfolio

By reading this document, the reader agrees that under no circumstances is the author responsible for any losses, direct or indirect, that are incurred as a result of the use of the information contained within this document, including, but not limited to, errors, omissions, or inaccuracies.

© Copyright 2021 - All rights reserved.

The content contained within this book may not be reproduced, duplicated or transmitted without direct written permission from the author or the publisher.

Under no circumstances will any blame or legal responsibility be held against the publisher, or author, for any damages, reparation, or monetary loss due to the information contained within this book, either directly or indirectly.

Legal Notice:

This book is copyright protected. It is only for personal use. You cannot amend, distribute, sell, use, quote or paraphrase any part, or the content within this book, without the consent of the author or publisher.

Disclaimer Notice:

Please note the information contained within this document is for educational and entertainment purposes only. All effort has been executed to present accurate, up to date, reliable, complete information. No warranties of any kind are declared or implied. Readers acknowledge that the author is not engaged in the rendering of legal, financial, medical or professional advice. The content within this book has been derived from various sources. Please consult a licensed professional before attempting any techniques outlined in this book.

Stock Market

Investing Guide for Beginners

Easton A. Ziegler

    How to Construct a Portfolio
        Choosing Between Investments
        When to Stay Away From Concentration
        Allocations
Chapter 5: Mistakes to Avoid
    Avoid Narrative Investing
    Avoid IPOs, SPACs, and Direct Listings
    Avoid Day Trading, Options, and Futures
Conclusion
References

Introduction

The stock market is a pretty big deal. Endless hours are devoted to analyzing its every move on financial and social media. There are so many ways for a person to make money in the market that it can be mind-boggling to the beginner. If you've ever wondered what the deal with the market is and why everyone seems to get hysterical about it, then you're in the right place.

There are many reasons for you to begin investing in the market. For starters, the stock market has been one of the primary wealth-creation machines in America over the past century. The stock market has posted an annual return of 10% every year since 1926 (Bainbridge, 2021). This period includes a bunch of market crashes and an untold number of company bankruptcies.

This period has witnessed the fall of giant institutions and the rise of new economic machines. The American economy has moved from a manufacturing-centered one to an information-based machine. However, the stock market has chugged along just fine throughout all of this, impervious to whatever has happened around the world.

Someone who invested $1,000 in the stock market back in 1926 would now have close to $10 million in savings. That's a pretty penny! Increase the amount invested to $10,000, and this person would be sitting on close to $100 million. This shows how powerful the stock market is and why ignoring it is one of the worst mistakes you can make.

Most people shy away from the market because of a general mistrust of the financial sector. I'll admit, it's hard to defend the actions of the average Wall Street firm and investment conglomerate. However, the stock market doesn't have much to do with the actions of these people. As you'll learn in this book, there are many ways of avoiding the damage that these actors cause to the economy and your portfolio.

My aim in this book is to give you a good grounding on sound stock market investment techniques. This isn't a book that is going to make you $1 million by tomorrow. However, follow the principles outlined in here, and making $1 million within 25 years is all but guaranteed.

The great thing about the stock market is that you can turn it into a passive wealth-creation machine. This is to say, you don't need to work actively to make money. Sure, you can devote time to analyzing the market, but you can also sit back and simply do nothing. The market will continue to make you money no matter what you do.

Passive, Active, and Everything in Between

The large number of ways in which you can make money in the market is both a blessing and a curse. On one hand, it's great to have a large number of options. However, the sheer number of options makes it easy to get distracted and chase the next shiny thing. Many investors fall into this trap and neglect sticking to a tried and tested method.

The truth is that there isn't a single good way to make money in the market. All the methods you read about work. Whether they'll work for you or not is the real question. Every investing method requires some combination of skill and mental discipline. This is why a method that works for one person will not work for someone else.

To make money in the market you need to stop chasing after a perfect method and instead ask yourself what works best for you. Are you an active or passive investor? Do you understand how odds and probabilities in the market work? Needless to say, these questions rarely strike beginners.

In this book, you're going to learn a lot more than just successful investing strategies. Your mindset will change once you're done, and you'll have a repeatable blueprint that you'll be able to scale and make money with no matter how much capital you have.

I must mention that, while any amount of capital is fine to get started, it's best to have at least $5,000 as investment capital before you begin. Capital of that size helps you invest in significant amounts, and you'll be able to scale your investments faster. However, if you don't have access to that much money right now, it's perfectly fine.

As you read this book, take the time to fully understand what is being conveyed. This is a very dense book in that I've packed a lot of information into a few sentences. You'll be learning about the way the stock market works, how successful investors approach the market, tried and tested principles that will make you money, and how you should approach the question of portfolio construction.

Many people arrive at topics such as these with preconceived notions. I urge you to let them go and instead follow the simple blueprint I'll give you in this book. Not only will you make money, you'll also sleep well at night knowing that your money is working for you with minimal effort on your part.

Take the time to read material that you believe you know all about. For instance, the first chapter deals with the basics of how the stock market works and the various actors that participate in it. You might think you know all about this or might be impatient to get to the strategies chapter.

I recommend reading the chapters in order, since each chapter builds on the previous one. Without understanding the basics of the stock market, you cannot hope to understand how a particular investment strategy works.

So, having said all that, are you ready to learn how to invest in the stock market? If yes, then let's move forward and dive into the nitty gritty of how the stock market works!

Chapter 1: How Stock Markets Work

Have you ever wondered why the stock market exists? What function does it serve in the economy? Does it even have anything to do with the economy? You'll often hear politicians take credit for how great the stock market is. Is there really any connection between political policies and the stock market?

This chapter is going to answer all of these questions and much more. For starters, let me make it clear that the stock market and the economy are two different things. There is a connection between them, but don't mistake a booming stock market for exceptional economic strength.

The years from 2009 to 2020 were a perfect example of this disconnect. This period witnessed the single greatest bull market (*bull market* is the term given to a rising market) that America has ever witnessed. Yet, the economy wasn't all that hot. Social unrest rose throughout the decade, and when the COVID-19 pandemic hit in 2020, there weren't too many people surprised at the damage that small businesses suffered.

Stock market prices are fueled by two things: emotions and fundamentals. In the short term, emotions are what move prices. For instance, people read about some news item on social media and immediately rush to buy shares. The price of that stock rises as a result.

In the long term, fundamentals are what drive stock prices. *Fundamentals* refers to the underlying business. The amount of money a business earns, the strength of its product, and so on are critical to stock prices over the long run. Think of short-term fluctuations as being a small part of a longer-term trend in the stock.

It's important to distinguish between the short and long term before we dive into the way the stock market works. The mindsets required to make either one succeed are very different. Many people confuse these mindsets and end up receiving middling to poor results.

Short Term or Long Term?

The average market participant views the stock market as a casino. They see bits of paper (or symbols) move up and down and try to get in on something hot. They completely neglect that those symbols represent real businesses, not some horse at a race track.

Short-term focus by investors in the market is often the result of a get-rich-quick mentality. People want to make as much money as possible, as quickly as possible, and chase jackpots. They listen to social media, their friends, their boss' brother-in-law's cousin, and so on in the hopes of gaining a hot tip they can use.

Success in the market doesn't come like this. It's extremely simple to get rich in the market. However, most people don't get rich because they don't have the right mindset. Instead of chasing jackpots, you need to knuckle down and focus on long-term investment (Bainbridge, 2021).

Investment implies long-term focus. You'll read many books where people talk about trading, penny stocks, and FX as being investment-related operations. This is not true. At its core, investing is about focusing on the fundamentals and trying to invest in assets as much as possible.

An *asset* is something that creates cash flow by providing value. For instance, a company generates cash flow by selling products that its customers love. By investing in that company, you're expressing a belief that its products are great and that its business is sound.

Another analogy that explains investing is to think of investing in a piece of farmland. If you had the opportunity to do so, your first move would be to figure out the crop yield that the land will give you and how much you can sell those crops for. Alternatively, you could lease it to a farmer and have them pay you a cut of profits.

You're highly unlikely to buy the land and then try to sell it to the next person in the hope of trying to make a quick buck. You're also not going to shop the land around trying to see what it's worth. However, so many people do this in the stock market. They buy stocks one minute and try to sell them the very next second in an attempt to capture minute price fluctuations.

This is a hard-brained way of trying to make money. How much can a stock rise in a few minutes or even days? In the introduction, I mentioned how the stock market has risen by an average of 10% every year since 1926. The best way to make money would have been to simply buy the market (let's assume you could do this) and simply hold on.

Compare this to the amount of effort it takes to jump in and out of the market, constantly trying to identify opportunities. By focusing on the short-term movements in a stock, you're effectively trying to predict the emotions that people feel towards a stock. How proficient are you at predicting emotions?

Can you predict the emotions of someone who is close to you all the time? Probably not. Then why do you think you'll be able to predict the emotions of millions of strangers? The thought is absurd! It's far easier to evaluate a company's fundamentals than it is to try to predict someone else's emotions about a stock.

Investment operations are based on rationality and aim to identify assets that will make you money over the long term. Short-term market operations are get-rich-quick schemes that rarely work. They rely on luck, and there's no way you can depend on luck in the long term. It's far easier to rely on skill and use that to make money.

Why Does the Stock Market Exist?

Now that you've understood that investing is a rational process, it's time to learn about the market you'll be operating in. The stock market is a vital tool that businesses use. Most market participants don't take the time to learn about the market, and this often sets them up for failure.

After all, if you don't understand the rules of the playground you're operating in, how can you expect to play the game well? The stock market exists for companies to raise capital for their businesses. Let's say you own a business and need cash to grow it. You have two choices.

First, you could borrow money from the bank or from investors. If you borrow money from the bank, you'll draw a loan and will need to make interest payments every month based on whatever interest rate the bank gives you. Borrowing from investors works the same way, except you'll "issue a bond" instead of drawing a loan.

Investors will give you money and buy your bonds that will pay them a certain interest rate until the bond expires. At that point, you'll repay them the money they loaned you when they bought the bond. Drawing a loan or issuing a bond is referred to as *debt financing*.

The second method of raising cash is *equity financing*. In this method, you'll carve out a portion of your company and issue shares in it. These shares will sell for a certain price in the market that investors can buy. Once they buy them, they're part owners of your company and have a claim on its profits and losses.

Notice the differences between equity and debt financing. Debt holders don't have access to company profits but instead get paid a fixed amount in a predictable fashion. Equity holders don't have any guarantees of making money, but the rewards they can earn are unlimited, since a business can grow to an infinite size.

The stock market makes it easy for companies to issue shares of themselves and for investors to buy those shares. Bonds are typically issued in the bond market, which is a completely different beast from the stock market. Since our focus in this book is on the stock market, all I'll say about the bond market is that it's dominated by large financial institutions, and the average small investor doesn't have to concern themselves with it.

Stock Exchanges

You might have heard of the term *stock exchange* previously. An exchange is simply a market where stocks are bought and sold. The New York Stock Exchange (NYSE) is an example of a stock exchange. Stock exchanges are private companies that make money based on the number of transactions that are carried out within them.

Typically, you'll find exchanges near major financial centers, such as New York or London. The Greater New York City area has as many as 12 stock exchanges. Most of these exchanges are behind-the-scenes operators and interact primarily with wholesale stock sellers.

Wholesale stock sellers are usually companies, investment banks, and clearinghouses. Investment banks typically manage the process by which a company can issue shares to the public. I'll explain shortly how companies do this. Clearinghouses are institutions that bear the most risk in the stock market, and yet, most market participants have never heard of them (Bainbridge, 2021).

These companies are the foundation on which stock exchanges are built. They help investors of all shapes and sizes execute their trades and make sure there's always a market for stocks that are fairly priced. If you log into your broker's software and place an order, it is a clearinghouse that makes sure you receive the stock immediately and at a fair price.

Returning to exchanges, they operate for a profit and are regulated by a number of bodies. In the United States, stock market regulation is intense, and this ensures that everyone has a level playing field.

Regulation

Regulation is a thankless job in many ways. No one commends regulators for preventing disasters, since the general public is unaware of these incidents. It's only when things go wrong that the regulators occupy the spotlight and everyone naturally thinks they keep screwing up.

However, this isn't true. Regulation is actually quite robust and is divided between three government agencies. The most famous of these is the Securities and Exchange Commission, or SEC. This body regulates the behavior of market participants. For instance, it makes sure that no one gains an advantage through insider trading or by trading with privileged information.

The SEC specifies a long list of rules that all companies have to comply with to remain listed on a stock exchange. This list includes the reports that must be filed at the end of financial periods and filings that indicate management and other insider ownership of stock in a company. The SEC makes all of this information available for free via its EDGAR website.

The second body that regulates the market is the Financial Regulatory Authority or FINRA. FINRA is responsible for licensing and making sure financial institutions play by the rules. For instance, FINRA regulates brokers and makes sure these companies adhere to the rules.

The third body is the Commodity Futures Trading Commission, or CFTC. The CFTC regulates all market activity in derivative instruments and FX. As such, we won't be covering anything to do with these market instruments. Let's just say that the CFTC has its hands full keeping track of the various ways in which people choose to create complicated financial products that invariably blow up.

Brokers

Your broker is your conduit to the stock market. Brokers are the target of many investors' ire, since there's a perception that they don't always play by the rules. However, this isn't the truth. The penalties a broker faces for swindling their clients is massive and isn't worth the risk. In the United States, all brokers are regulated by FINRA.

It's impossible for a small-time investor to trade directly with the exchange, since exchanges prefer dealing with wholesale stock sellers and buyers. Therefore, it's impossible for you to avoid a broker. Brokers have a fiduciary duty to execute your trades and no more.

They're not there to provide you financial advice or to help you make sense of the market. Don't mistake this as them trying to deceive you. The average broker makes money when you trade, and this is their primary concern. The less you trade, the more unpopular you're going to be with the broker. However, this doesn't mean they'll try to steal from you.

Most brokers these days offer commission-free accounts. This means you won't pay fees to trade stocks. However, nothing in the markets is truly free. These commission-free brokers sell your order information to large hedge funds, who then sell stock back to you at a small markup. Therefore, you pay for stocks one way or another. This practice of selling order flow is called *payment for order flow*, or PFOF.

As unfair as it sounds, it's fully legal. Most stock exchanges make their money through PFOF as well, and it's deeply ingrained in the financial system these days. The only way to prevent PFOF from hurting you is to avoid short-term trading where you jump in and out of the markets constantly. This is yet another reason why a long-term, investment-minded focus is so important.

You'll incur lesser costs and will be able to make money more easily. For now, let's return to brokers. All brokers are connected to a clearinghouse that executes all of their trades. The relationship between a broker and a clearinghouse is quite simple. The latter executes trades and assumes market risk for which the former (the broker) has to deposit collateral.

Once trades are settled (usually in two business days), the risk meter is readjusted to zero. As a brokerage client, you won't have exposure to this process. You'll simply click a button, and you'll receive stock in your account immediately. The behind-the-scenes work that a clearinghouse does is what ensures this happens.

When choosing a broker, make sure you pick one that treats the market as serious business. App-based brokers don't always do this. They push you to trade complex financial instruments by appealing to the get-rich-quick mindset that is deeply ingrained within all of us.

Choose a broker that doesn't inundate you with free stocks or with trade ideas. Remember, your broker exists to execute your trades. They're not financial advisors, and it isn't their job to help you make money. Making money is your job, and as you'll learn in this book, it's nowhere near as difficult as it's often made out to be.

Instruments

The stock market offers a wide variety of instruments that you can use to make money. Stocks are the most commonly found instruments, and you've already learned about bonds. Most brokers will also allow you to trade derivatives. A *derivative* is a financial instrument that gains its value from another instrument.

For instance, options derive their value from the stocks upon which they rest. If the stock price rises, the option's price rises. There are also options that rise in value if the stock price falls. Generally speaking, derivatives are perfect get-rich-quick instruments. I mean to say that they can make you a lot of money quickly.

As a result, they attract many people who want to shortcut their way to riches. The problem is that they're powerful tools. When they go wrong, they can wipe you out completely. This is why derivatives tend to create outsized losses when things go wrong. Uninformed market participants jump into derivatives believing they'll make a lot of money but inevitably get burned.

It's best to stay away from derivatives. You can start trading them once you've gained enough market experience and have fully done your homework on them. When used the right way, derivatives, such as options, can make you money. However, you need skills to utilize them.

For now, understand that the stock market offers you many ways of making money through the vast number of instruments that exist. It's tempting to want to use complex strategies to make as much money as possible. However, simplicity is what wins in the market.

Operating in instruments you don't understand is a surefire way of losing money. Be smart, and stick to the simple stuff. Over time, you'll gain experience and can expand the types of instruments you invest in.

Chapter 2: The Five Principles of Intelligent Investing

Most beginners to the stock market dive right into it and focus only on learning strategies. They focus on choosing instruments instead of understanding that their mindset and approach to the market is what determines their success. Here's something you need to understand: No strategy in the world can fix a poor mindset.

Besides, strategies are something that short-term traders focus on extensively. This is because they need to choose the right indicators, read market conditions accurately, and then predict short-term moves. As an investor, your approach is different. You're not concerned with what the market does on a daily basis.

The way to make money through investing is deceptively simple. All you need to do is identify your investment approach (active versus passive), choose the right instrument for this approach (individual stocks versus passive instruments), and then hold on for as long as possible.

Of course, a lot goes into choosing the right stock if you're going to be an active investor. However, picking these stocks isn't as much about strategy as it is about understanding what you're investing in. You'll need to figure out what the business is about and behave as if you're buying a portion of the business for yourself.

After all, this is what stock ownership signifies. You're not buying a piece of paper. Instead, you're looking to create an asset by investing your money. This asset will give you cash flows and capital gains (a capital gain occurs when the price of an asset such as a stock rises) well into the future.

Active investing is a tough task, and not many people pull it off. This happens because most people get bogged down by the numbers and try to analyze everything under the sun (*How the Stock Market Works*, 2019). For instance, they try to figure out a technology company, then switch to a natural resources business, and then flit over to a consumer-goods business, and so on.

No one has the ability to understand every single business on the planet. This is just one example of a mistake that most aspiring active investors make. What you need is a set of guiding principles that will help you quickly unearth promising companies that you can then dive deeper into.

Let's look at the first principle now.

The First Principle

The overarching rule governing investing is that you should not lose money. To be precise, you should do everything you can to avoid losing money. Therefore, all behaviors and situations that pose a significant risk of loss ought to be avoided. A natural conclusion of this broad rule is that you should stick to investing only in what you know and understand.

This is the first principle of successful investment. Don't bother investing or even trying to invest in something that is incomprehensible to you. For instance, if you understand a consumer-goods business and don't understand technology, don't invest in technology. This sounds very simple, but most people ignore it.

The reason for this is the fear of missing out. After all, most market participants spend their days reading about how this stock is going up and how that sector is poised to rise to the moon and so on. They think they'll miss out on huge gains by sitting on the sidelines and will miss out on the chance to get rich.

The media makes it seem as if everyone is getting rich by investing in these stocks, and it's easy to fall prey to this delusion. If everyone else is getting rich, it's natural to want to jump in as well. So, what's the real problem here, and does sticking to what you know while ignoring everything else work?

We can understand this principle better by considering a simple analogy. Everyone (and everything) on this planet has skills they're naturally predisposed towards. If you're in the ocean and see a fish, you're not going to judge its ability to be a fish by asking it to climb a tree. Neither will you expect a lion to survive for very long if you asked it to swim in the ocean.

We understand this intuitively. Staying within the boundaries of our expertise is something we do in real life all the time. Just because you can drive a car on the highway reasonably well doesn't mean you're ready to jump into a racecar and compete in motorsport. The thought doesn't even occur to most of us.

Yet, when it comes to stock market investing, everyone becomes an expert in everything. Using intelligent sounding words like "beta," "volatility," and so on, we try to identify the "best" stock instead of figuring out which businesses we understand. Much like a fish trying to climb a tree, we invest in things that we don't comprehend simply because we think the price of that stock will rise. Is it any surprise that we'll receive fish-trying-to-climb-a-tree results by doing this?

The right move is to identify what you're good at and stick to it repeatedly. In the context of the stock market, this means identifying businesses you can understand. Remember, these aren't pieces of paper that can be interchanged. Amazon's stock is a very different beast from Facebook's stock, which in turn is very different from Google's stock.

These companies are in the same sector, but they're very different businesses. It's perfectly fine to understand one business and admit that another is incomprehensible. Admitting what you don't know reduces the risk of you losing money to it. You might be thinking that you don't know anything about business right now.

Well, this is where education comes into play. You've learned about the SEC's EDGAR website that provides all corporate filings for free. Begin by reading the annual filings of companies, and proceed from there.

Every company files an annual report called the 10-K which explains their business in great detail. It also lists the risks and management's thoughts on the business.

Crucially, the SEC mandates strict guidelines that companies have to follow with regards to the language they use in these reports. In contrast to PR and news releases, companies cannot dress up poor results in flowery language. They have to be direct and explain things as they are.

Reading 10-Ks is the easiest way to educate yourself. Don't take my word for it. Warren Buffett, widely regarded as the greatest investor ever, has always said that he spends at least five hours every day reading 10-Ks and that they've helped him increase the size of his expertise (Schroeder, 2008).

If you're working at a day job, begin by looking at your employer's 10-K. See if you truly understand what the business is about. Look at their competitor's 10-K. See if you can spot any differences. Can you figure out which is the better business? Don't worry about stock prices and performance. Look only at the way the cash flow works for these businesses.

Look at how management discloses information and identifies risks. How do they allocate capital? The 10-K has a section called the Management Discussion and Analysis (MD&A), which is full of useful information. Spend a few hours reading 10-Ks, and you'll automatically come away with a better understanding of how a business works.

All of this requires work, and this explains why most people shy away from it. They'd rather opt for easier solutions, such as hot stock tips or believing that a few lines on a chart can predict which way prices will go. It takes work to identify good businesses. Stick to what you understand, and constantly educate yourself.

It's the only way to achieve investing success.

The Second Principle

While the first principle deals primarily with choosing the types of companies you should focus on, the second focuses on how long you should hang onto your investments. Ideally, you should never sell your investments. I understand that this statement might create confusion (Leeds, 2021).

After all, the common narrative surrounding stock investing is that you buy something, wait for it to rise, sell it for a profit, and repeat the process. However, this ignores the overarching rule surrounding investing: to avoid losing money. By repeatedly buying and selling stocks, you'll increase the costs associated with investing massively.

There's another problem with jumping in and out of the market. It's almost impossible to consistently identify great opportunities. For instance, if you managed to invest in Amazon stock back in 2007, you'd have a significant sum in your portfolio. Would you rather hang onto your investment or would you rather invest it in the next Amazon?

Undoubtedly the second option seems more attractive. However, ask yourself, how often do companies like Amazon come around? The 2000s were a unique decade in that we witnessed the rise of a new sector as the American economy turned digital. This seismic shift resulted in companies such as Amazon, Google, Netflix, and Facebook turning into multi-billion-dollar corporations.

Can you recall any company from the 1990s achieving this? Or how about a company that went public in 2011 (excluding Facebook)? Chances are that these lists will be sparsely populated. This is because such exceptional companies come by very rarely. Even if they do come by, identifying them at an early stage is tough.

For instance, would you have invested in Amazon back in 2007? The company had been earning a profit for only a few years despite all the hype, and it was still rolling out its Prime service. Amazon was still viewed back then as a bookseller first and retailer second. No one knew anything about AWS, which is the beating heart of Amazon's business these days. There certainly wasn't any talk of cashierless stores, robots replacing humans in warehouses, and drone deliveries.

Most importantly, every other retailer was transforming themselves into an online seller. Giants such as Macy's, Sears, and Target had begun building online sales outlets, and there was intense competition in the purely online space as well with Overstock.com, Bluefly, etc. joining the party. In the middle of all this, it was impossible to say how Amazon would have fared.

Another great example is Facebook. Back in 2007, it wasn't the world's favorite social media company. In fact, it didn't even have a monetization plan. It was just a place where people posted pictures of themselves. Yahoo was considered a stronger company, Google had its own social media network, and there was Myspace. Myspace these days is a poster child of how to ruin a great opportunity, but back then, there was no telling how these companies would fare (Leeds, 2021). Social media wasn't even a thing.

It's easy to look back from the present moment and think you could have identified these great companies. However, when you examine the events at the time, you'll see that they were not sure things. Ask yourself: Can you identify a future trillion-dollar corporation right now that is worth less than a billion dollars?

You might have a few guesses, but it's impossible to predict such things with any certainty. My point here is that thinking you can jump from one great stock to another is unrealistic. The smart thing to do is to identify great companies and then stick with them through thick and thin.

It takes time for companies to grow substantially. Amazon has been one of the fastest-growing companies in history. However, it was founded back in 1995 and went public in 1997. It took Amazon at least 13 years to become a credible business and a pillar of the world's economy.

If the fastest-growing company took 13 years, you can imagine what the average time looks like. Generally, a company needs at least 20 years to achieve significant growth. If your idea of investing is to hold a stock for a week and then find something else, this should help reorient your focus.

One of the reasons growth takes a while is due to the way compounding works. Compounding is a mathematical phenomenon where a sum of money grows exponentially over time. This is opposed to linear growth. Let's look at an example of both.

Let's say you have $2, and every day, you receive an additional $2. By the end of five days, you'll have $10 ($2, $4, $6, $8, $10). Notice that this growth is linear. Your money grows by a fixed amount every day. In percentage terms, your growth declines every day. The first day, you receive 100% gains ($2 in gains while you have $2 on hand).

The second day, this decreases to 50%, 33% on the third, 25% on the fourth, and 20% on the fifth. What if we change this up a bit and assume that your percentage gain remains the same throughout? That is, you receive 100% gains every day. What would your gains at the end of five days look like then?

Day 1 → $2 + $2 = $4

Day 2→ $4 + $4 = $8

Day 3 → $8 + $8 = $16

Day 4 → $16 + $16 = $32

Day 5 → $32 + $32 = $64

This is an example of an exponential gain powered by compounded growth. $2 turns into $64 at the end of five days thanks to this. Compare this to the $10 you receive through linear growth, and you can see how powerful compounding is. In this example, I've assumed 100% returns every day, which is extremely unrealistic.

In real life, you'll see companies grow at 12–15% annually. Over time, these gains add up to significant amounts. If you invest $5,000 in such a company, you'll have $81,832 at the end of 20 years (assuming 15% growth). This is pretty impressive by itself, but you might be thinking that $81,832 is hardly a sum that qualifies you as rich.

Well, this is where reinvestment over time and the power of compounding come together to work their magic. Let's say you invest $1,000 per month ($33 per day) over those 20 years, in addition to your initial investment of $5,000. At the end of 20 years, you'll have $1,311,155.

The lesson here is consistency and discipline cannot help but make you rich. You don't need fancy strategies or secret indicators to get rich. Neither do you need to constantly identify great opportunities. All it takes is a few opportunities and repeated investment into them to make you rich. That's the power of $33 invested every day.

Think about this the next time you spend $33 on frivolous expenses. Can you muster $33 every day and put it into an investing account? You probably can. I'm not saying you should deny yourself luxuries. However, it certainly does put investing and getting rich into a new light. All you need is $33 invested every day for as long as possible. Compounding and time will make sure you end up with at least $1 million.

The Third Principle

While compounding can make you rich, there's still the question of finding the next great opportunity. The truth is that great companies don't come by very often. Even if they do, they're hard to spot. However, there are a few telltale signs of great companies that are easy to spot.

The first sign is the presence of an economic moat. A moat was something that medieval lords built around their castles to protect themselves from invading armies. The idea was that, by digging a ditch around the castle and filling it with water, alligators, and other unsavory things, opposing armies would think twice about attacking a castle.

It also meant that the entry points into the castle could be controlled by simply retracting the bridges over the moat. In short, it gave the castle an unfair advantage in battle. We don't have marauding medieval armies these days. However, in the world of business, competition and technology have ensured that companies need to constantly adapt and deal with challenges.

This means that, to survive over the long run, businesses need an inherent advantage that helps them repel competition. An economic moat gives the businesses greater probability of thriving over the long run. So, what does an economic moat look like? There are many forms it comes in.

The most recognizable moat is a strong brand name. Coca-Cola, Johnson & Johnson, Ferrari, Armani, Louis Vuitton, and so on have strong brand names that people all over the world recognize. If you were given a choice between drinking Jimbo's Cola and Coca-Cola, you'd definitely pick the latter, even if both concoctions tasted the same.

A strong brand name gives a company a large raft of advantages. For starters, it ensures greater sales through increased recognizability. Second, it reduces the impact on sales that economic downturns create. I've listed a bunch of luxury brands above, but everyday companies also benefit from great branding. For instance, Nike and Walmart tend to do well, even in downturns.

If anything, the likes of Walmart and Costco do better in downturns, since they're viewed as places to purchase cheap groceries at all times. Remember that a strong brand is something that a company's customers easily recognize as being an authority. It doesn't necessarily have to be famous.

For instance, most people wouldn't have heard of American Data Processing, or ADP. However, ADP is one of the strongest brands in the world. If you receive a paycheck, odds are that ADP has processed it. Large companies around the world (ADP's customers) know what ADP is extremely well.

Similarly, you might not have heard of Moody's. This company provides investment ratings for bonds and other securities that trade in the financial markets. However, financial institutions know Moody's very well. In fact, Moody's, along with Standard and Poor's, have a duopoly when it comes to the investment-ratings business.

There are other forms an economic moat can take. For instance, size is an economic moat. Walmart is so large that it forces suppliers to reduce their prices to rock-bottom levels. Amazon does the same thing with its competitors. It's so large and well-capitalized that it can afford to lose money on sales purely to wipe competition out and establish market dominance.

Technology companies benefit from a large number of users being active on their platform. For instance, Google's algorithm gets better the more it's used. The more people search for stuff, the better it becomes at predicting what people are searching for, what their speech patterns are, etc. This means search results get better, which fuels even more activity, and so on.

Patents and copyrights are a great source of economic moats. For instance, Pfizer holds as close to a legal monopoly as possible in the erectile-dysfunction market thanks to Viagra. Everyone knows that Viagra is thanks to the patent that Pfizer holds, in addition to the moat the brand name alone generates. Note that brand power in this case was the result of a product that delivered what it promised.

Viagra's formula cannot be copied easily thanks to the patent that Pfizer holds on the product. While the patent has expired in large parts of the world, Pfizer still holds majority market share thanks to the credibility the drug has built.

When looking at a company, your task is to examine what kind of an economic moat a company has. More often than not, you'll find that the company doesn't have one. For instance, Tesla is often hyped up as a great stock. While it's a great company, does it have an economic moat?

Evidence says no. Tesla's battery technology isn't much different from what other manufacturers produce. Its cars don't have greater range than a comparable luxury or budget EV from another manufacturer. Its autopilot and ludicrous mode have been hyped, but Mercedes Benz developed the first autopilot system back in 2003 with the S-Class.

Ludicrous mode has always existed in sports cars and sedans, cloaked as power boosts and special settings. In fact, the German car manufacturers have entire brands devoted to ludicrous mode–like features (AMG Mercedes, BMW's M division, Audi's RS cars, Porsche, and Lamborghini in the case of Volkswagen).

Tesla doesn't have any sustainable advantage when it comes to battery production either. It lacks the capital base that established manufacturers have. Overall, other than a mythical brand name, there isn't much going on here in terms of a moat. This doesn't mean Tesla is a poor business.

However, its odds of success are low over the long run. Again, this doesn't mean it won't succeed. However, when making predictions, all we can do is take odds and probabilities into account. An economic moat increases the odds of success significantly. You can never expect a sure thing in investment, but lining the odds in your favor will yield better results than hoping on luck to pull you through (Little, 2021).

Note that, 20 years from now, if Tesla does succeed, it doesn't make this prediction "wrong" or "miscalculated." It doesn't change the fact that it lacks a moat and that the odds are stacked against it. Thinking in terms of results doesn't work in the markets. You need to think in terms of probabilities.

You're not "missing out" on anything you don't understand or whose odds of success were low to begin with.

The Fourth Principle

As a shareholder, you own a piece of a company. You have the right to ask questions about the direction that the company is taking and how well its management is running the business. However, from a practical standpoint, it isn't as if you can have the CEO on speed dial and call them whenever you like.

Most corporations these days ensure that the general public has limited say in company matters. They do this by issuing a different class of stock than the ones they own. Pretty much every share available on stock exchanges lacks the voting power that shares owned by company insiders do.

As a result, you need to be extremely sensitive to the quality of a company's management. You're completely dependent on them to deliver results to you. Therefore, in addition to evaluating the quality of a business, you need to evaluate its management as well. There are a few signs you can look for when doing this.

For starters, look at the kind of people the CEO surrounds themselves with. CEOs occupy an outsized importance in the American business landscape. They often come across as superhumans. However, the fact is that multi-billion-dollar, or even multimillion-dollar, corporations cannot be run by a single person.

Even mythical founders have strong teams backing them. For instance, Steve Jobs often came across as being the only person involved in everything to do with Apple. However, this ignores the contributions that Steve Wozniak made in the early days, Jony Ive's design inputs that created Apple's iconic products, and the steady support that Tim Cook provided Jobs with.

In addition to this, the list of former Apple employees who went on to do great things at other companies is a telling sign of the high quality of people Jobs surrounded himself with. Apple's ranks were deep, and it explains why the company has continued to thrive even after his death.

Similar patterns exist at Facebook despite that company not being anywhere near as loved as Apple. The list of former employees who have gone on to achieve great success and the presence of a number of strong voices within the company indicate that Facebook has a deep roster of management it can draw from in times of crises. Mark Zuckerberg occupies the spotlight as founder and CEO, but he's surrounded by management that backs him up ably.

Outside the technology sector, companies such as JP Morgan Chase, Walmart, Ford, and Disney exhibit the classic signs of deep management rosters. Examining what former senior management did after leaving the company is a great sign. Looking for signs of CEOs giving credit to their employees by name is also a good sign of a CEO who recognizes the importance of high-quality management.

The best companies are run by teams of people, not a single rockstar. Therefore, if you spot signs of megalomania in a CEO, chances are that this person doesn't surround themselves with people that challenge them. The company might do well for as long as the CEO is present, but once they leave, expect things to deteriorate.

You can also pick up clues from the MD&A section in the 10-K filings that the company makes. Look at the history of comments made by the management, and evaluate them for transparency. For instance, if you know that the company had a crisis a few years ago, read the 10-Ks from those years and a few years prior to that. Notice how the management looked at the business and whether they had any inkling of what was about to happen.

At the end of the day, evaluating management is a subjective effort. Some qualities will appeal to you, while those same qualities might turn someone else off. This is perfectly fine. What you want to do is exercise your opinion of the company through stock purchase. Everyone's opinion is different, and this is fine (*Stock Market Guide: What Is the Stock Market and How Does it Work?*, 2021).

One red flag to watch out for is a CEO who hogs the limelight for no discernible reason. If a CEO spends most of their time on Twitter than on running the business, it's a pretty bad sign. Management that is extremely concerned with the company's stock price and routinely attacks short sellers (people who bet on the company's stock price to fall) is another red flag.

A company's stock price has no material impact on its underlying business. The only thing it affects is management's ego and their compensation. Many CEOs and high-level executives have compensation tied to the stock price. If it dips below a threshold, they get paid less. Therefore, if CEOs start chirping (tweeting) about the stock price, you can bet this is because they're putting their pockets ahead of business results.

The Fifth Principle

While the previous principles are important, this fifth principle is what ensures you'll always be successful. It ties directly to the biggest rule of investing, which is to avoid doing things that lose you money. It's called the *margin of safety*, and it's a rule that every successful investor practices.

So, what is the margin of safety? Interestingly, it isn't a financial concept. The margin of safety comes from the field of engineering. When designing things like bridges and buildings, engineers make a ton of estimates. These estimates deal with the stress limits of materials, the amount of strain they can bear, maximum shearing forces, and so on. While these numbers have been tested in laboratories, they're still estimates, since no one can accurately replicate on-site conditions in a lab.

The more complex a project is, the greater is the number of estimates that have to be made. These estimates can cascade into a large error tolerance built into the design. Therefore, engineers have to account for the possibility of error before finalizing their designs. They do this in a deceptively simple way.

Once they complete their calculations, they multiply the final result by two, or some number. It's a pretty easy hack when you think about it. If you're uncertain about something, simply double your result to ensure that you'll be safe. It's a rule that will protect you immensely when investing.

Successful investing is about making sure the odds are on your side and not against you. Remember, you'll never find certainty in the markets. No one can accurately predict which way the market is going to go.

Successful investors protect themselves from risks at all times.

The first way to protect yourself from risk and build a margin of safety is to invest money that you can fully afford to lose. If you're investing your life savings or money that you need to pay monthly bills, you need to stop doing this. Sure, you might hit the jackpot and end up making a lot of money. However, the odds are against you.

It isn't the final result but the odds that count. Think of it this way. Let's say you're planning your monthly budget and are trying to figure out how much you can afford to spend on certain categories every month. For simplicity's sake, let's assume you have just three categories, rent, food, and entertainment, and that your income is $1,000.

If you fix a threshold of $500 for rent, $300 for food, and $200 for entertainment, you haven't left much room for errors. What if you encounter an emergency or have to pay for an expense in bulk instead of monthly? These thresholds make it tough for you to be flexible.

However, if you reduce your rental expense to $300, you've given yourself a buffer of $200. If you reduce the threshold for the other two categories by $100 each, you've now given yourself a buffer of $400. You have a margin of safety that amounts to $400. Even if you go over the thresholds on certain categories, you'll still have enough cash in your margin of safety to protect yourself from running out of money.

Also note that building a margin of safety into each category builds your overall margin of safety. This is the approach you must adopt when it comes to constructing your portfolio. If you invest in three companies, you must build a margin of safety within all of them.

Following the previous four principles ensures you have a qualitative margin of safety. If you understand the company, and it has a significant economic moat, along with good management, your odds of success are pretty good over the long run. A final margin of safety that you can add to your stock purchases is to buy the stock for a price lesser than what it's worth.

If someone offered you the chance to buy something worth $2 for a dollar, you'd take that deal without second thought. Why not do the same with the companies you buy? Note that I'm not saying you should pay a 50% discount at all times. Just make sure you're receiving a bargain as much as possible.

A margin of safety on price ensures that you can absorb a decline in stock prices to a greater extent than someone who pays an inflated price. The question is, how do you figure out what price to pay for a company? Financial theory defines a method called discounting future cash flows to calculate net present value as the best way to figure out what a company is worth.

The problem with this method, aside from it being a mouthful to pronounce, is that it requires a lot of estimates that are tough to define. A better way, even if it's less accurate, is to use a shortcut via the *price-to-*

earnings ratio (P/E). The P/E ratio is calculated by dividing a company's stock price by its earnings.

If you flip the P/E ratio (let's call this the E/P), you'll receive the yield on the stock. Yield is a measure of the return you receive on your investment. If you invest $10 in an asset and it gives you $1 per year, you receive a yield of 10% ($1/$10).

From an investment perspective, the earnings that a company makes is a measure of the ROI you would receive if you owned it outright. Once you understand a company well, you can figure out how much it expects to grow its earnings every year. Most companies will grow their earnings at their historical rates.

Let's say a company is growing its earnings by 10% every year and is currently earning $2 per share. Let's also assume that the P/E ratio throughout remains the same (in reality, it will increase if the company remains profitable, since other investors will jump in and increase demand). Finally, let's assume the current share price is $20 (P/E ratio is 10).

The E/P of this stock is (2/20) 10%. 10% is the market's average rate of return, and it isn't all that attractive. To earn this return, you could simply invest your money passively and do nothing else. Therefore, to qualify for an investment, you can specify an E/P threshold of at least 12%.

This means the price of this stock has to decline to at least $16.60 before you would consider buying it. If you buy it at that price, you'll be earning a yield of 12% on your money. This calculation assumes that P/E will remain the same, and if you've been following along, you'll see that this builds a margin of safety into our calculations.

If a company performs well, its P/E usually rises. However, by assuming it doesn't rise, we're assuming the worst-case scenario and are working from there. This means, even if the investment doesn't work out as planned, we've paid a low enough price for the company and can absorb a few blows.

This method isn't perfect and oversimplifies a lot of things. However, unless you want to dive deep into complex financial theory, it's the best way of figuring out how much to pay for a stock. Note that you'll still need to understand the business and develop some confidence in the numbers you project.

I'd also like to point out that a low P/E ratio doesn't automatically indicate a cheap company that is a good investment. Great companies often sell at high P/E ratios. This doesn't make them poor investments. If you're faced with a high-P/E company, the thing to do is to figure out how much its earnings will increase by every year. If the earnings growth rate is greater than 12–15%, then it makes sense to invest in it.

This brings to a close our look at the five principles of successful investing. As you can see, these points are more mindset related than related to a technique or strategy. Active investing requires a lot of work and a ton of research. It requires you to spend a lot of time investigating businesses and reading their reports.

Throughout the process, make sure you understand the odds of success and always ensure they're on your side. Without this, you won't have much of a chance.

Chapter 3: The Best Passive Investing Strategy

As I mentioned in the previous chapter, active investing takes a lot of time and dedication. Most people won't have the time it takes to make it a successful venture. After all, between a day job and other demands that life places on us, it's impossible to carve out enough time to successfully analyze a business.

This doesn't mean active investing is a doomed pursuit. If you're truly passionate about the markets, then you'll manage to make time. However, what if you aren't passionate about the markets and simply want to see your money grow? Well, that's where passive investing comes into the picture.

Passive investing, as defined in this book, is investing your money periodically into a reliable investing vehicle and doing nothing else. Sounds pretty simply, and it really is easy to execute. You'll have to stay out of your way and avoid jumping in and out of the markets, as with active investing. However, passive investing doesn't require you to do anywhere close to the amount of research that active investing demands.

Passive Investing Origins

The idea of passive investing has always been around, but it was only until the 1980s that it became a reality for ordinary investors. The underlying thesis of passive investing is that, as long as the American economy remains prosperous in the long run, its companies and the stock market will continue to rise.

History has borne out this fact. From 1926 till the present day, the S&P 500 (a stock market index that I'll explain shortly) has returned 10% every year on average. The S&P 500 is an index that captures the performance of the 500 largest companies in America. The inclusion criteria are quite simple.

A company has to be one of the 500 biggest in America and has to trade a certain volume on the reputed stock exchanges. In case there's a deadlock, the company that has maintained its status for longer is given priority. The first index to come into existence was the S&P 500 back in 1926. It began life as an index that consisted of the 26 largest companies and morphed into its current version in the mid-1950s.

Throughout its existence, the index has risen onwards and upwards, reflecting American economic prosperity. Mind you, in the short term, the index has diverged from what's been going on in the economy. However, over the course of time, it's managed to accurately reflect how great the economy has been.

It's important for you to recognize that the stock market and the economy are two different things. I mentioned this earlier as well. Over a decade or two, it's very likely that they'll diverge. However, over long enough timelines, there will be some correlation.

Examining the S&P 500's evolution in this regard is instructive. At its inception, the index consisted mostly of steel companies and railroads. In the 1970s, financial companies began entering the index, while railroads had long since dropped out. By the 1990s, financial companies were the majority, and internet companies started entering the index.

These days, technology dominates the index, while financial companies have taken a backseat, even if they haven't fallen out of favor just yet. The point here is that the index has automatically screened in the best and biggest in America automatically. To understand which sectors are doing well right now, simply take a look at the index, and figure out which sector has the most companies in the S&P 500.

Another fact to note is that, as the size of the American economy has grown, so has the index. Thanks to increased prosperity, the average size of an American company has grown substantially. Back in 1926, a $500-million company was considered massive. These days, Amazon and Apple are worth $1 trillion, while $500 million is considered "small."

As a side-note, when you hear talk of the size of a company, understand that the market capitalization is being discussed. The market cap is calculated by multiplying a company's share price with the total number of shares it has issued. The market cap isn't an indicator of a company's business prospects. However, it will tell you how much more growth it has left in the tank. A trillion-dollar company can only grow so much. However, a $500-million company has a considerable runway ahead of it.

Returning to the index, it should be clear by now that one of the best investing strategies over the past century would have been to simply buy whatever was in the index and hold onto it as long as the company was present in it. The minute a company dropped out, investors could have sold it and bought whatever replaced that company.

Many professional investors did exactly this back in the 1930s. However, ordinary investors were unable to use this tactic because the costs associated with it were great. Trading-commission costs were too large to justify purchasing 100 or more stocks in a portfolio. Tracking them daily was also a headache, since the percentage allocations had to match the index. For instance, if stock A was one percent of the index, it had to be one percent of your portfolio. This meant investing took a lot of time, and it was mostly clerical work.

Lastly, there was the issue of capital. Assuming even distributions of capital between all stocks in the index, an investor with $1,000 would have to spread it amongst 500 stocks. This means each stock would receive $2 each. Most stocks don't sell for that low, which makes the strategy unviable.

An index wasn't a security that could be traded, so there was no way to simply buy the index or a representative of it. All of these issues existed until 1976.

The First Passive Investing Instrument

1976 witnessed the creation of the first investing vehicle that would allow ordinary investors to partake in the American economy with a single purchase. It was called an *index fund*, and it was created by John Bogle and his company, The Vanguard Group. Bogle's idea was ridiculed by professional investors at the time.

However, his idea was sound in nature thanks to its simplicity. Investors would buy units of Vanguard's fund, and in turn, Vanguard would purchase all stocks present in the S&P 500 in proportions as they existed in the index. As a result, investors received exposure to all companies in the index with a single purchase.

However, the real benefit of Vanguard's approach was that the company didn't need to charge hefty fees. All it was doing was copying an index. It wasn't trying to outperform the market or do anything special. It looked at what was on a list, bought it, and maintained it. This meant management fees were low, and investors could keep more of their money.

Management fees are a high hurdle to clear for most investors. The average mutual fund, which is a managed investment fund, aims to outperform the market. The investment manager actively manages money to find great stocks to invest in. However, they charge fees for this expertise which can run as high as two to three percent of capital invested.

What's more, the average actively managed mutual fund underperforms the market (Bainbridge, 2021).

Yet, fees are still charged. This means the manager makes money no matter what, while the investor has to hope for extraordinary outperformance every year to make money. Index funds changed all that.

They taught investors and the broader financial community that aiming for the average was perfectly fine. As long as the American economy remained solid and business conditions were great in this country, investing in a broad American stock market index was a great strategy.

These days, many indexes exist. You can invest in an index that tracks technology companies, housing companies, real estate, foreign stocks, Chinese stocks, Chinese tech stocks, Chinese non-government-owned tech companies, and so on. The vehicle that enables this is the index fund. Exchange-traded funds (ETFs) are also a good vehicle for these objectives.

An ETF is similar to a mutual fund in that it has a manager and a defined investment objective. Like mutual funds, many ETFs are actively managed, and many of them underperform the market. The difference between an ETF and a mutual fund is that ETFs trade like stocks do. Their prices fluctuate regularly as investors buy and sell them. Mutual fund prices don't fluctuate during the day. They're fixed at the end of a market session, and that's what they trade for the following day.

Many ETFs track indexes like mutual funds do. When it comes to index funds and ETFs, the only difference is that ETFs don't have minimum investment requirements. Most index funds will ask for a minimum investment of $3,000. ETFs are, therefore, a good option to get started.

What Should You Track?

Once you enter the world of passive investing, it's easy to get carried away with all of the options available at your disposal. It's best to keep things simple and stick to indexes that cover the broad stock market. This way, you're getting a piece of American business across the board and won't have to worry about one sector failing or another rising.

ETFs and index funds also make it easy for you to get a piece of American real estate. When researching individual stocks, you'll come across certain companies called real estate investment trusts or REITs. These companies own real estate and collect rental income from those properties.

Thanks to their corporate structure, these companies pay 90% of their income back to their shareholders. They do this so as to avoid paying corporate income tax to the IRS. For investors, REITs are a great tool, since they provide cash flow as well as capital gains.

However, investing in individual REITs is as risky as investing in a stock. After all, REITs are still companies, and you'll have to analyze their business as you would any other business. Therefore, to mitigate this risk, you can invest in an index that tracks REITs. Vanguard, iShares, and other prestigious fund issuers have a number of passive funds that track REIT indexes for low costs.

While all index fund fees will be low, some are lower than others. Vanguard typically charges the lowest fees of all fund issuers, with an average cost of 0.06% to 0.1% of total capital invested. Other fund issuers, such as iShares, Barclays, Nuveen Asset Management, and SPDR, tend to charge higher fees, but even these average between 0.06% to 0.2%.

When choosing funds, stick to the fund issuers I've mentioned above. These companies have been around for a long time and have reputable asset managers. In addition to them, Charles Schwab and Fidelity are also good fund houses. When picking funds, it's best to stick to the largest ones.

Size matters in the passive investing world. Typically, funds greater than $5 billion in size are considered safe. Size is important because investor withdrawals can increase the trading fees that a fund has to pay. These funds minimize their brokerage and transaction fees thanks to volume discounts. If their assets under management decrease, then their fees increase, and this will be passed onto you.

Trading costs are one of the reasons why a fund will not fully replicate its index's performance. Every index fund will lag a little bit. Choose a fund that minimizes this lag. Usually, it'll be around 0.1–0.5% in terms of performance. Note that you should minimize your fees as well. A fund that has minimal lag might charge much higher fees than one that has a slightly greater lag.

Pick the best combination of the two, along with size. The final piece of advice here is to repeatedly invest in the fund. Keep investing money every month, preferably as much as you can, and don't touch the fund. It'll grow on its own, and you'll eventually have a huge nest egg to live off of.

Generating Cash Flow

One of the knocks against stock market investing is that you can't use your investments to pay your bills. To put it precisely, stock investing doesn't generate cash flow that you can use to reduce your monthly expenses. The majority of gains are capital gains where the price of the asset increases over time.

While capital gains are great, they're mostly on paper. You can't encash those gains until you sell the asset. This means you won't have cash flow until you sell. What if you could exchange some of those capital gains for steady cash flow? Active investors can do this by selling a small portion of their holdings every year to replicate a cash payment from their stocks.

However, passive investors don't have the time or the inclination to figure out how much to sell and so on. Instead, it's far better to invest in dividend-paying stocks and dividend-tracking indexes. A *dividend* is a cash distribution that a company makes to its shareholders. Remember how REITs pay their shareholders 90% of their profits? Well, that's a dividend.

Dividend-paying stocks are great because they're usually stable companies that have excess cash. You'll find that well-established companies, or companies that are in stable businesses without having to worry too much about competition, pay regular dividends. Dividend stocks are also great because they tend to decline less during market downturns thanks to the cash flow they give their investors.

Despite this, investing in a dividend-paying stock requires time and research. The risks are pretty much the same as investing in a normal stock. What if the company stops paying a dividend? What if it goes bankrupt? Therefore, passive investors are better off focusing on indexes that track dividend stocks.

When it comes to dividends, there are two major indexes that you can choose to track. The first is the Dividend Aristocrats index, and the second is the Dividend Achievers index. The Aristocrats index is composed of companies that have regularly raised their dividend payments for at least 25 years.

While the threshold is 25 years, the majority of the companies in this index have maintained and raised their dividend payments for close to 50 years. Examples of these companies include Coca-Cola, Altria (you might know of them as Marlboro), and Kimberly-Clark (Huggies diapers, Scott toilet paper rolls, etc.).

These companies are behemoths in their industries and face very little competition. The flip side is that there isn't much growth left for them to achieve. After all, how much bigger can Coca-Cola realistically get? Unless

Martians start drinking the stuff, Coca-Cola has hit its peak in terms of size or is very close to it.

Thus, the steady dividend cash flow that these companies provide is offset against the fact that their stock prices rise at slightly lower rates than the average market does. However, when times are rough, they don't fall as much. Therefore, they manage to achieve market-average performance over the long term.

They're boring stocks to hold, and the Aristocrats index is equally boring. However, it's stable, and you'll manage to sleep well at night. In contrast, the Achievers index offers a little more excitement, but in a good way. The criteria for an Achiever is for a company to maintain a steady stream of dividend payments for at least 10 years.

Quite a few Aristocrats make this list, but by and large, the list is populated with companies that have more runway to grow and are hitting their stride as major corporations. This means the dividends they pay are lower than what an Aristocrat might pay, but they make up for it by providing greater capital gains to their shareholders.

However, the flip side of this excitement is that the Achievers list is slightly more volatile than the Aristocrats list. It changes more often, since companies fall out all the time. Therefore, an ETF or index fund that tracks it will incur greater trading fees. As a result, the fees you'll pay are greater. However, it's not as if the fees are exorbitant.

You'll still pay around 0.05% as management fees when you track this index. There might be greater lag in the index funds, so you must look at minimizing this when choosing a fund. All the major fund issuers mentioned previously have ETFs and index funds that track the Achievers index as well as the Aristocrats.

More conservative investors will find the Aristocrats a better bet. The Achievers are also a good bet if you want good capital gains in addition to your steady income. Note that REITs are typically not added to these indexes. You can purchase a REIT index fund from the issuers mentioned previously.

The dividend yield (calculated by dividing the dividend payment by the price of the fund) of a REIT index fund is usually greater than a stock index fund. However, the stock fund will deliver more capital gains. Therefore, whichever way you slice it, you'll end up achieving average market returns. In the case of the American market, the average is a very good place to be.

There are index funds that track foreign stocks as well, but their record is patchy. For instance, China has been talked about as a great power, and the country has reached the status of a developed nation. However, the index fund that tracks the Chinese market (issued by iShares) has remained flat throughout the previous decade (2010–2020).

Some of the other index funds that track different sectors in the Chinese economy are risky. For instance, the funds that track Chinese tech stocks (a highly hyped sector) are extremely volatile. There are other obscure

ETFs that track equally obscure indexes that jump up and down all the time. A 30% gain in one year is erased by a 20% fall the next.

It's best to stay away from such volatile performance. Stick instead to tried and tested investments, and remain invested for as long as possible. I'd previously mentioned that it's ideal to never sell your investments. You might have wondered how you could then enjoy the fruits of your nest egg.

Well, dividend investing makes this possible. Once your portfolio reaches a seven-figure value, you can invest your money into a dividend-paying fund that yields around three percent, which is a very realistic yield percentage (good margin of safety in this assumption!).

Let's say your final portfolio value is $2 million. Three percent of that amount every year is $60,000, which is $5,000 per month in passive income. Increase your monthly contributions to your investment account while you have active income, and you can increase your passive income when you retire. Pass your portfolio onto your heirs, and let them enjoy the passive income as well.

Best of all, if you never sell your investments, you'll never pay capital-gains taxes on your portfolio. You'll pay ordinary income taxes according to your tax bracket on dividend income, but you'll manage to retain the bulk of your principal over the long term. Just another reason why you ought to remain invested for as long as possible.

Chapter 4: Building a Portfolio

Portfolio building is an important skill that you must get right if you want to use the stock market to achieve financial freedom. Sadly, many investment gurus neglect providing advice on this topic because it's a bit dry and boring. Most market participants neglect this as well for the same reason.

Much like eating your vegetables when you were younger serves you well into adulthood, you need to understand the basics of portfolio creation and management to succeed. The good news is that it's pretty straightforward to create a portfolio the proper way.

What's tough is sticking to this disciplined approach. Also, your choice of active versus passive investing impacts the way you go about building a portfolio. Let's examine these differences now.

How to Construct a Portfolio

When you set about the task of buying stocks or index funds for your portfolio, your first choice is to decide whether you want to sink all of your money into one particular instrument or whether you'd like to spread it out between multiple purchases. Another way to frame this argument is to ask whether you'd like to concentrate your portfolio or diversify.

Both approaches have their merits. A concentrated portfolio will always deliver the highest gains, but it also has the potential to go the other way and generate outsized losses. A diversified portfolio will cushion losses, but it won't move as high as a concentrated portfolio will either.

So, what is one to do? Well, the answer is quite simple. If you're going to be an active investor, concentration is the way to go. If you're going to be a passive investor, then diversification is where it's at for you. Why am I framing these choices in terms of your strategy?

An active investor is looking to outperform the market at all times. This is why you'll be investing in individual companies and analyzing their businesses. It takes a lot of work, and you want to make sure you're well compensated for your effort. This means loading up as much as possible on a good thing. Remember that great opportunities won't come by very often.

For example, if you'd figured out that Amazon and Google were going to be great investments back in 2006, would you have wanted to diversify away from them? I don't think so! You would have wanted to put everything you own into those two companies. If you had done so, you'd be a multi-millionaire by now.

Many active investors diversify away from their core investments because they try to hedge their risk. They think that, by spreading money across a few unrelated investments, such as gold and silver, they reduce their risk. This is the wrong way to think. It reduces risk on paper, but it reduces reward dramatically as well.

If you're worried about the risk of failure once you've invested in a company, then your analysis is at fault, not your portfolio. If your analysis is incorrect, you're going to lose money anyway. No amount of money placed in gold or alternate assets is going to make up for it. In fact, if you're right about the company, you'll only hinder the gains you make.

In short, this is acquiring the worst of all worlds. You'll lose money when things go wrong, and you won't make as much as you can when they go your way. When you choose to invest actively, you're going to have to become comfortable with the risk that comes with this pursuit. Think of it as the risk of doing business.

If you cannot find ways to deal with this risk, then perhaps passive investing is a better choice for you. The best way to deal with the fear of being wrong is to create a checklist of what you think are the reasons to invest in a company and compare them to the reasons to stay away from it. If you've prepared well and have conducted a thorough analysis in accordance with the principles you've learned in this book, then you should be fine.

Besides, building a margin of safety into your investment reduces the impact being wrong will have on your gains. The margin of safety is what protects you, not diversification. If you're going to spend a lot of time analyzing companies, concentrate your portfolio into your investments, and make sure you get paid when things go right.

Choosing Between Investments

Let's say you've identified a great company and have invested all of your capital into it. While the stock does its thing, you begin amassing more capital and are on the lookout for other great companies. Let's say you find one. You now have a choice. Should you sink capital into the existing stock, or should you buy as much stock of the second company as possible?

Active investors face this question all the time, and it's an important one to answer. Should you stick to the known good investment, or should you extend your portfolio to another company? Adopting a rational approach to this question is the best way to move forward.

For starters, can you enter the first company at a good price? A good price is one that gives you a good margin of safety. Remember that, no matter how great a company is, you need to always maintain a margin of safety in case things go wrong. Even Nostradamus needs a margin of safety in the markets, so you definitely could do with one.

If the margin of safety is present in the first stock, your next task is to identify which stock will give you more growth. In short, which is the better investment? This is a tough question to answer. It might be best to split your capital between the two if this is the case.

If the margin of safety isn't present in the first stock, then investing all of your capital into the second (at a good price) is the way to go. Continue to do this with all of your investments, and you'll build a portfolio that is safe and optimized for growth. As a side note, you'll read a lot about growth investing versus value investing.

The margin of safety approach is typically associated with value investing, while growth investing is presented as a rollicking ride where you pay expensive prices for fast-growing companies. This isn't quite true. The fact is that even growth investors (as they're called) are investing in value.

They believe that their companies will grow to become more valuable and are ultimately paying a price that they believe is lesser than what the company is worth. They're paying a nickel to buy a dime, much like value investors are. Growth and value are the same thing when you're investing in a quality business. Don't get caught up with these artificial categories.

Simply look for great companies, and allocate your capital as I previously described. A pertinent question to ask is: Should you sell? Ideally, you shouldn't. However, we don't live in an ideal world.

Therefore, I'll just say that you should look to sell only when the fundamental reasons you invested in a stock don't hold anymore. Perhaps the business changed, or you're not a fan of the new management. This is when you should sell and stick that money into your existing investments at good prices or new ones if you've located some.

If you haven't located any, then stick the cash in an interest-paying account, and sit tight. Keep looking for opportunities to enter at good prices or for new businesses. When the moment occurs, pull the trigger, and deploy your capital.

Interestingly, this is exactly how CEOs make the decision to allocate capital within their companies. You're the CEO of your investment business, so follow this framework at all times.

When to Stay Away from Concentration

Portfolio concentration is the way to go if you're an active investor. However, if you're going to be a passive investor, then diversification should be your method of choice. Why is this? Simply put, you don't know or don't have as much expertise as an active investor does.

Your goal is to make money in as risk-free a manner as possible. This is why you'll be investing in index funds after all. From a high-level perspective, the best way to mitigate risk in a situation where you're unsure of results is to spread your risk as thinly as possible. This way, you'll minimize negative results while achieving positive results that are about average.

This is what an index fund does for you. Each of these funds contains around 100 stocks at the very least. With a single purchase, you've diversified your money across many different baskets. However, you need to go beyond buying just one fund. You need to think about economic sectors as well. This is why it's a good idea to buy at least two funds for your portfolio.

The first fund should be a broad-based stock market fund (that pays dividends or not), and the second should be real estate focused. This way, you'll manage to gain exposure to the two pillars of the American economy: business and real estate. For most investors, this level of diversification is more than enough. With two purchases, you'll manage to capture all of America's prosperity.

Some investors make things worse by buying bond funds, foreign stock ETFs, alternative investments, and so on. These investments have their place depending on your goals. However, the average investor will do perfectly fine without them. Let's begin by looking at bond funds and whether they have a place in your portfolio.

Bond funds track bond indexes and pay dividends to their unit holders. Generally, bond funds pay a pretty good yield, somewhere around 4%. However, they don't rise in value too much. The average bond fund has provided investors with 5% returns since 1926 (Bainbridge, 2021). This is half of what the stock market has given investors.

The rationale behind investing in bond funds is to protect your portfolio in case the stock market declines. Historically, the bond and stock markets have moved in roughly opposite directions. However, thanks to changes in central bank policy and the way financial institutions trade these days, the bond market has become less uncorrelated to the stock market. As a result, bonds have become a good way to generate income in a portfolio but don't provide protection from capital losses.

Foreign stocks have always held allure for investors. The idea of investing in some unknown Swedish company that becomes a media darling has been a popular narrative that is hard to resist. The reality is that most foreign companies and stock markets are extremely unreliable. I've already highlighted an example of how a high-growth market, like China, has produced less than satisfactory results for investors.

This doesn't mean that foreign stocks don't have a place in your portfolio. However, you should think about owning them only when your portfolio's value exceeds seven figures. At those levels, allocating between 5% to 10% of your funds to foreign stock ownership makes sense.

The same advice applies to alternative assets, such as cryptocurrencies, gold, silver, oil, and so on. In fact, other than cryptocurrencies, gold, and silver, you shouldn't even think of investing in anything else. Oil, soybeans, corn, and so on are commodities that have supply and demand cycles of their own. You'll need to research them thoroughly, just as you would any other stock. Obviously, if you're looking to invest passively in the market, this isn't a practical course of action.

Don't allocate more than one percent of your portfolio to alternatives, and do so only when your portfolio reaches seven figures. The Bitcoin craze that's currently gripped the world doesn't have any foundation in investment principles. It's a bunch of people chasing money trying to get rich quickly.

There are many intelligent-sounding arguments for Bitcoin and cryptocurrencies as investments, but at the end of the day, none of them makes much sense. For instance, inflation is often pushed forward by crypto enthusiasts as a reason for legitimacy. However, hyperinflation of the kind that crypto evangelists talk about is unlikely to occur in the world's developed economies.

The most damning argument against crypto is that it can never be used as a means of daily transaction. For this to happen, the value of the average cryptocurrency has to be equal to the dollar, roughly. Much like how the Euro and the Japanese Yen trade in tight bands around the dollar, cryptos will need to be worth around the same. Where does this leave BTC and its ridiculous $60,000 valuation?

BTC was the first crypto to come into existence, but there have since been better currencies that have minimized BTC's weaknesses. If those currencies really are better, then why is BTC valued much higher than them? ETH sells for a few thousand, while BTC sells for high five figures. How does this make sense? If investment principles were truly driving prices in the crypto market, we'd see currencies valued according to their utility.

However, this clearly isn't the case. Therefore, stay away from crypto. You can afford to risk a miniscule portion of your portfolio on it once you have enough money. Until then, don't worry about what BTC or any other fancy coin is doing.

Allocations

The average passive investor needs to buy just two funds to achieve optimal diversification. The proportion in which you buy these funds depends on your investment goals. For instance, if you want to prioritize income generation, then you can invest more into dividend-producing funds or REIT funds.

If capital gains are your objective, you can invest more into broad stock market funds. Generally speaking, it's a good idea to have at least 60% of your portfolio in stocks and the rest in real estate. If you want to generate income, then invest in a dividend stock fund. This way, your entire portfolio will produce income.

Irrespective of whether income is your priority or not, make sure you choose to reinvest your dividends via a dividend-reinvestment plan, or DRIP. DRIPs are free of cost, and they allow you to buy fractional shares of your funds, which is something that isn't possible if you're looking to buy fund units outright.

The way DRIPs work is quite simple. You check a box on your broker's software to indicate you'd like to participate in a DRIP. Your broker will automatically start reinvesting your dividends into your existing funds. If your stock fund pays a dividend, your broker will buy as many units as the dividend can buy.

Note that your broker will reinvest your dividends in their entirety. You'll still have to pay taxes on those dividends at the end of the year depending on your marginal tax bracket. Your broker will give you a form at the end of the year that indicates how much you were paid. This form is called the 1099-DIV. You'll need to use this information when filing your taxes.

Does it ever make sense to opt out of a DRIP and receive cash into your account? It does when your portfolio is substantial enough to generate enough cash for you to live on and if your goal is to live on passive income earned. However, for the most part, it makes sense to simply reinvest your dividends. You'll boost your compounding immensely, since your investments will be paying for themselves.

To conclude our look at portfolio construction, make sure you diversify or concentrate according to your investment objectives. Passive investors should buy in accordance with their income-generation goals. Stay away from fancy investments, and keep it boring and simple. It's the best way to make money.

Chapter 5: Mistakes to Avoid

Thus far, I've talked about all of the things you should do to make money in the stock market. What about the things you shouldn't do? Well, that's what this chapter is going to be about. There are many schemes and fancy strategies that promise huge rewards in the market. However, few of them work, and it's easy to get lost in a maze of complexity.

Without further ado, let's look at the mistakes you should avoid at all costs in the market.

Avoid Narrative Investing

Narratives are everywhere in the stock market. Human beings love stories, and the media, be it mainstream or social, loves selling us fancy investing schemes in the form of narratives. One day it's EV stocks, the next it's 5G, the third it's Chinese AI, and so on. All of these investments might have their merits, but my point here is to avoid buying into an overhyped sector or narrative.

In fact, it's a good idea to stay away from financial media of all kinds because most of these people are paid shills at the end of the day. Wall Street analysts receive a ton of attention, but these professionals aren't exactly unbiased. The average analyst will never hit a huge company with a sell rating because that will effectively destroy their career.

The analyst business deserves a closer look, since it highlights everything that is wrong with the modern financial institution. An investment bank is a large organization that has many different departments. Broadly speaking, there are three functions that these companies execute. The first is to take companies public via a public offering of stocks. The bank earns hefty fees for doing this and earns a profit by selling the stock as well.

The second is trading their own money and providing brokerage services for their clients. This is a murky world where the bank often trades against their clients or simply acts as a regular broker and stays out of the transaction. Investment banks provide brokerage services to institutions that usually speculate in the bond and FX markets.

These markets aren't governed by the same laws that the stock market is governed by. In the stock market, a broker is not allowed to trade against their clients. Such rules don't exist in the bond and derivative markets, making them a free-for-all. Banks often assume positions in companies and financial instruments tied to companies that could make them money. However, there's the possibility that these positions could go against them as well.

This brings us to the third business function, which is to provide advisory services. This branch is where analysts work, and on the surface, these people research a company and provide recommendations for a fee. However, it isn't as simple as that. Regulators have long since noticed that the trading divisions and advisory divisions have a conflict of interest.

What if a trader on a bank's bond desk holds an outsized position that they want to get rid of? How hard would it be to get an analyst to prescribe a sell rating on the stock, which will increase demand for the bonds and allow the bank's trader to get out of a losing position? Not very hard at all, one would think.

In response to this, banks have crossed their hearts and pinky sworn that their analysts and traders don't talk to one another. These banks have long fallen back on the term "Chinese wall" to indicate the separation of business functions. Aside from being oblivious to the racial connotations of that term, the thought that an investment bank adheres to an ethics boundary between departments is laughable.

History has repeatedly shown that these ethical boundaries don't exist. Prior to the dot-com crash in 2000, many Wall Street analysts pushed buy ratings on internet stocks that fueled their prices to astronomical levels. In the aftermath of the crash, regulators discovered that not only did these analysts own significant quantities of the stocks themselves, their companies were often tasked with taking these dot-com companies public.

It was a classic case of one division helping the other out at the expense of the public. Regulation forced greater separation after that incident, but concerns remained. The market crash of 2007–2009 highlighted the impossibility of the situation. While one side of a bank was pushing toxic securities to customers, the other side was quickly unloading them. The thought that top-level executives didn't know this was happening or didn't engineer this situation is laughable.

The point of all this is: Don't trust Wall Street analyst ratings. Even if you ignore the ethical problems with the business, there are other issues, such as company access. A large company provides a great deal of access to analysts with an implicit expectation that the analyst will provide them a favorable report.

If an analyst slaps a major company's stock with a sell rating, they can kiss their career goodbye, since no one else will give them the access they need to do their jobs. An investment bank has no use for an analyst that doesn't play ball. After all, advisory services are a cost center at a bank and exist to serve the money-making investment banking and trading arms.

The financial media is an extension of these analysts. Read prominent financial publications, such as Barrons, and you'll notice how every journalist talks about this analyst's recommendation and that one's. There's very little focus on what is actually taking place in the market, and these so-called journalists miss the forest for the trees.

Their newsletters and social media are full of intelligent-sounding nonsense, like "Here's why the Dow fell by 100 points" or "What Netflix's fall means for long-term bondholders" and so on. Stocks rise and fall every day. There's no need to get hysterical about it.

One sympathizes with these journalists because, if they followed reporting guidelines according to sound investing principles, they wouldn't have much to write about. All they do instead is get paid to make noise. Ignore them, and you'll be just fine.

Avoid IPOs, SPACs, and Direct Listings

The need for easy money drives investors towards all kinds of investment schemes. Chasing after initial public offerings, or IPOs, is a common mistake. An IPO is a process by which a private company goes public. It's when a company first issues shares to the public.

Typically, the IPO process is handled by an investment bank (a model citizen of the financial world if there ever was one) that helps the company file a wide range of paperwork that helps it comply with exchange regulations. The nature of these regulations isn't important. All you need to know is that going public is a serious business, and companies have to step up their game with regards to disclosures material to the business.

As part of the deal, investment banks charge hefty fees. In addition to this, because too much money is never a concern for these folks, they also seek to profit from the stock listing. The investment bank, or promoter as they're referred to, buys a huge block of stock or buys warrants on it. Essentially, the promoter "guarantees" a certain price to the firm by telling them that the bank will buy the stock at a certain minimum price and provide a floor for the stock in case it goes into freefall.

Next, the promoter markets the stock to large institutions and hedge funds. These people buy stock in bulk and can provide hefty trading volumes that will make the stock attractive to the wider public. Eventually, mentions of the stock find their way onto analyst reports, as described previously, and on mainstream financial media.

When the day arrives, the stock price predictably surges as the promoter begins cashing out, along with the company insiders to a certain extent. The large investors who invested money before the IPO (through venture capital) cash out and earn hefty returns. The people buying these post-IPO shares are usually institutions and common investors.

Large institutions have huge balance sheets and fixed criteria that govern their investing process. It seems odd to say this, but making money isn't always their goal. Risk mitigation is. As long as perceived portfolio risk is low, their investors don't care too much about how small their returns are. This is not the case for an ordinary investor.

Typically, IPO shares pop upwards and then fall back down to more sober levels. By that point, the investment bank has cashed out and made its money, leaving you holding the bag. If the company happens to be something like Facebook, you'll be fine. If not, you're going to lose money.

The decade between 2010 and 2020 has witnessed a bull market like never before. A clear sign of overheated bull markets is the presence of nonsensical IPOs. This pattern has held true. Companies that didn't have a hope of earning a dollar until exceptional events arrived (Zoom) went public on mere promises. Note that this isn't a commentary on Zoom's business. It's merely an example of how a company that never made money went public anyway until it lucked into a global pandemic.

For all its faults, the IPO process does reduce the number of terrible companies that go public. There's a lot of paperwork, and investors scrutinize financial reports. The bull market craze has, however, given us a new financial vehicle called a special purpose acquisition vehicle, or SPAC, that allows companies to circumvent the IPO process.

In short, if you're in a hot sector and can coherently put together a single page of hopes and dreams, you can become a billionaire using the investing public's money. This is pretty much what every EV maker has pulled. A SPAC isn't a new invention. It's been around for a while but has only now reached manic levels.

The idea is simple. A well-known promoter with access to large investors forms a shell company (the SPAC). They announce that they're going to look for companies that belong to a certain sector (EVs, 5G, enter your own buzzword). Large investors buy shares of this company for a few dollars, and the promoter goes public with this company.

They then approach private companies in their chosen sector and convince them to merge with the SPAC. Since the companies are conducting a mutually agreed upon merger, the private company doesn't have to undergo IPO scrutiny. They immediately go public, the share prices rise based on hopes and dreams, and the promoter either sells their shares or hangs onto them while pocketing a bonus from the formerly private company.

The fact that celebrities have become affiliated with SPACs tells you all you need to know about how robust the process is. It's just marketing at the end of the day and is a way to separate you from your money. A solid, profitable private company doesn't have anything to fear by going public. It's the get-rich-quick scam artists that have no substance that need such vehicles.

In case you're wondering, yes, investment banks are involved in the SPAC process. No bank worth its salt will let a money-making opportunity pass by unexploited. The bank helps the SPAC go public and makes introductions to private companies.

Given all of these shenanigans, a direct listing seems almost innocent in comparison. This is a procedure where a company opts to list its shares directly on the exchange and cut investment banks out of the deal altogether. It's a risky move, since there's no floor established on the stock. However, if the company is strong enough, there's no risk of the stock falling sharply.

Coinbase, the cryptocurrency exchange, went public via direct listing in 2021 and experienced good results. Given that it was a profitable company to begin with, this choice made sense. From an investor's standpoint, though, direct listings are still risky because of the pop that occurs.

If everyone wants to get on board a great company, its shares will rise to a level where you won't have a margin of safety. This makes them risky and volatile to invest in. It's best to let things settle down and then see if the company warrants an investment.

Avoid Day Trading, Options, and Futures

At some point, every market participant wants to make more money and thinks they can succeed at day trading, swing trading, or FX trading. They start looking at options and their ability to generate income and marvel at how simple options are. Futures are another area that attract many investors because they allow you to effectively own a stock without paying all the cash required upfront.

It's natural to be drawn towards these instruments and methods. However, the fact is that, aside from options, all of these methods have a high failure rate and will only increase your costs of participating in the market. You're, therefore, going to create a high hurdle for yourself, and it's unlikely you'll overcome it.

Speaking of options, they are wonderful instruments, but they're also very easy to get wrong. Think of them as powerful tools that you need to fully understand before handling. If you don't understand them well, you'll end up hurting yourself. In financial terms, you'll end up wiping yourself out.

Options allow you to leverage your positions. This is to say, they allow you to control more stock for less money. Many brokers these days push their clients to trade options by positioning them as being easy to trade. Tesla's stock went through a manic phase in 2020 where uninformed investors kept buying Tesla options at high prices, and the stock kept rising, thereby making them money.

However, this money was a result of luck, not skill. These people didn't understand anything about the business and their entire investment thesis boiled down to "Elon is a god-Twitter-Troll-Shorts-#Elon4EVA." The fact that they made money isn't really relevant. They'll eventually end up donating it back to the market.

Adopting a structured path to trading options is the intelligent way to go about it. Educate yourself as to how they work and how they can augment your investment process. Don't trade them for the short term. Instead, use them to generate income in your portfolio.

There are a few options strategies that can provide you with a safe income stream. However, it takes time to master these, so don't rush into them. Also, understand that your degree of activity will increase once you choose to do this. Therefore, make sure you fully understand what you're getting into.

Conclusion

The common thread underlying all of the mistakes in the previous chapter is making decisions based on emotional cues instead of relying on rationality. Emotions are ever present in the markets, and it's naïve to think you'll be able to get rid of them. Instead, it's far better to be conscious of them and notice when they bubble up and distort your thinking.

Investing successfully is much simpler than you think it is. The problem is that most people just can't get out of their own way. They insist on complicating the process, thinking that complexity is what brings results. However, as every successful investor knows, simplicity is what brings results.

Keep things simple with everything you do. Don't try to overcomplicate stock selection, and always return to the basic principles you've learned in this book. Don't think that greater activity in the market is what makes money.

This is far from the truth. In fact, low activity reduces the costs associated with investing, and it makes it more likely that you'll keep your gains. As I've shown you in this book, creating a portfolio that is worth a million dollars or more is simple. If you follow the principles outlined in here, you can't help but end up with that sum in your portfolio.

What you need is patience and the ability to ignore your mind's propensity to fall for get-rich-quick schemes. Most people think that a single huge gain is what builds great wealth. However, in reality, it's a series of small events compounded that builds wealth.

Always keep thinking in terms of odds and probabilities when it comes to evaluating investments. Don't fall for common narratives peddled in the media, and always do your own research. You know much more about business than you currently think! Sure, it takes work to figure out what makes a business tick, but it's worth the effort.

Follow the portfolio-construction guidelines I've written about in this book, and you'll manage to create a wealth-building tool that will serve you for a long time. I'm positive that the information in this book will help you achieve your dreams. Let me know what you think by leaving me a review.

As a final piece of advice, remember: Stay patient, and build your skills. Luck will automatically find its way to you!

References

Bainbridge, J. (2021, April 20). *Long-term Investing: Avoiding the Volatility Game | J.L. Bainbridge.* JL Bainbridge. https://jlbainbridge.com/blogs/long-term-investing-and-avoiding-the-volatility-game/

How the Stock Market Works. (2019). The Balance. https://www.thebalance.com/how-does-the-stock-market-work-3306244

Leeds, P. (2021, April 20). *How to Dive Into Investing Without Having Fear.* The Balance. https://www.thebalance.com/8-steps-to-overcome-investment-fear-4101564

Little, K. (2021, April 20). *Why You Should Invest in Stocks.* The Balance. https://www.thebalance.com/part-one-the-stock-market-doesn-t-care-about-you-3141062

Schroeder, A. (2008). *The snowball : Warren Buffett and the business of life.* Bantam Books.

Stock Market Guide: What Is the Stock Market and How Does it Work? (2021, April 20). NerdWallet. https://www.nerdwallet.com/article/investing/what-is-the-stock-market

www.ingramcontent.com/pod-product-compliance
Lightning Source LLC
Chambersburg PA
CBHW070813220526
45466CB00002B/650